Martin McCardie

DAMAGED GOODS

First published in 1994
by dualchas
1/R, 21 Garturk St., Glasgow

ISBN   0 9521418 1 7

British Library Cataloguing in Publication Data
A Catalogue Record for this book is available from
the British Library

Printed by Clydeside Press, 37 High Street,
Glasgow.

The publisher acknowledges subsidy from the Scottish
Arts Council towards the publication of this book.

Special Thanks to

Robbie Jarvis
(We worked together on an idea, "The Patriot
Game", which eventually became "Damaged
Goods")

and
to
Wiseguise Productions

For Maureen, Erin and The McCardie's

First Production

DAMAGED GOODS was first presented in its original form at the Arches Theatre, Glasgow on April 14th 1992 with the following cast:

MICHAEL O'HANLON ------------ Brian McCardie
JEREMY SMITH -------------------- Allan Henderson
THE WOMAN --------------------------- Maureen Carr
Directed by Jim Twaddale

Second Production

DAMAGED GOODS was first presented in its present published form by Wiseguise Productions at the Citizens Theatre, Glasgow on 30th November 1993, with the following cast:

MICHAEL O'HANLON -------------- David McKay
JEREMY SMITH -------------------- Allan Henderson
THE WOMAN -------------------- Kathy-Kiera Clarke
Directed by Jim Twaddale

Production Manager ---------------- Aileen Robertson
Music ------------------------------------- Gary Grochla
Set Design ------------------------------- Suzanne Field
Lighting Design ---------------------------- Paul Sorley
Stage Manager ------------------------- Maureen Dalton
A.S.M. ------------------------------------- Drew McKay

Act One

The action takes place in a disused Scout hut near Liverpool Docks. The hut is in obvious disrepair. There may be faded gymnasium lines on the floor, or something to show that some form of training once took place there. There should be various boxes and pieces of rubbish thrown around the room. It is important that the boxes can be used to sit on. There should be only one entrance/exit to the scout hut. In the opposite corner from the door are a pile of rags, that could only be used for bedding, there is also a half eaten tin of beans, and several empty cans lying around.

There are three characters in the play, MICHAEL O'HANLON, A young Scotsman dressed in jeans and a leather jacket, he has a green white and gold scarf wrapped around his face. He is holding a handgun.

Jeremy Smith is a young middle class Liverpudlian dressed in a cadet's uniform. He is carrying a small shoulder bag .

The woman is in her early twenties. She is from Derry. She is shabbily dressed and looks in dire need of a bath.

As the lights go down gentle Irish music is heard. The music finishes and there is a pause...........the door bursts open and MICHAEL throws JEREMY on to the middle of the floor. JEREMY cowers in terror; for one moment MICHAEL points the gun at JEREMY, looks as though he may shoot him. He then looks round the room and rushes round placing objects against the door, trying to barricade it. After this he's knackered and leans breathlessly against the wall. JEREMY is still terrified and watches MICHAEL like a frightened rabbit. There is a long uncomfortable silence ......eventually JEREMY attempts to speak...............

JEREMY. Please........I don't know what I've done........

      MICHAEL runs over to the cadet and points the gun at his head

MICHAEL. **Shut up.......Shut it!** Make another sound and I swear to god, I'll blow your fuckin head off. **Right!**...........do you hear me?
JEREMY (terrified). Alright........alright.

      MICHAEL backs away from the cadet... watching him. The one is as scared as the other. There is a long uneasy silence.

MICHAEL. What is this place?

      JEREMY doesn't answer. MICHAEL approaches him.

MICHAEL. I said...what is this place?

Again JEREMY doesn't answer him. MICHAEL points the gun at him.

MICHAEL. Answer me ya wee shite you're making me lose my temper.

JEREMY. Sorry...sorry. It's just that a minute ago...you said you'd shoot me if I made another sound, that's all.

MICHAEL. Oh smartarse are we? In the mood I'm in, I don't appreciate funny men.

JEREMY. I wasn't being funny....honest.

MICHAEL. Shut up ya sarcastic shite, this isnae a kid-on....I'm serious.....you'd better believe how serious I am.

JEREMY. Sorry.

MICHAEL. What?

JEREMY. Sorry.

MICHAEL. What did you say?

JEREMY. I just said, I was sorry.....like.

MICHAEL. Sorry! I fuckin hate sorry. Sorry gets right oan ma tits.

JEREMY. I was just trying to...

MICHAEL. My Granda taught me never to say sorry. "Say sorry..and ye become sorry" That's what he told me.

JEREMY. Sorry......I mean, oh god I don't know what I mean.

MICHAEL holds the stare for a moment, then

looks around the hut.

MICHAEL. Where am I?

JEREMY. Eh....it's the old scout hut.

MICHAEL. The old what?

JEREMY. It's the old scout hut..they moved out not that long ago...they had to stop using it because of the roof.

MICHAEL. What's wrang wi' the roof?

JEREMY. It leaks.

MICHAEL. Oh.

JEREMY. And all the tiles are unsafe.

MICHAEL. Right.

JEREMY. Apparently the walls are set to come down any time.

MICHAEL. Aye alright...alright. I don't need the whole fuckin history. I just wanted to know where we were. Just sit there and shut it.....right.

MICHAEL moves around the hut becoming familiar with his surroundings, checking for potential escape routes, etc. After a while JEREMY speaks.

JEREMY. Excuse me?

MICHAEL. What!..what is it?

JEREMY. Nothing.

MICHAEL. What is it?

JEREMY. Nothing honest. Nothing.

MICHAEL. I'll decide if it's nothing. Now what is it?

JEREMY. It's a stupid question...never mind.

MICHAEL. I'll decide if it's a stupid question or no...now what the fuck is it?

JEREMY. Well....you said that your grandfather told you never to say sorry to anyone.

MICHAEL. Aye that's right , and I never have, not since I wis a wee boy.

JEREMY. Never...no matter what the circumstances were?

MICHAEL. Never!

JEREMY looks puzzled then turns away and gently shakes his head

MICHAEL. What do you want to know that for?

JEREMY. It's not important really.

MICHAEL. Oh **really**....well if you don't **really** tell, I'll **really** boot yer balls.

JEREMY. It's just...well I find it hard to believe that there would **never** be a situation where someone had to say sorry to someone else.

MICHAEL. Aye, but I'm no just anybody. My Granda taught me...I'm special. You said sorry to me ten times in one sentence..that's the difference.

JEREMY. That's what I mean.

MICHAEL. What?

JEREMY. It depends on the circumstances.

MICHAEL. What are you on about?

JEREMY. Well..you might have said sorry, if your

circumstances were a bit more like mine .....
you've got the gun, so I'll say anything you want.

MICHAEL. You are a fuckin smartarse....just keep
your mouth shut.

JEREMY. Sorry.......I mean...

MICHAEL. Just shut it.

*MICHAEL paces around the room like a
trapped animal. JEREMY quietly watches him.
Suddenly MICHAEL stops.*

MICHAEL. Shite! Does this place have a
nightwatchman?

JEREMY. I'm not sure; it did have one. He might still
come for all I know.

MICHAEL. Oh no!

Pause. MICHAEL thinks.

JEREMY. Excuse me.

MICHAEL. What?

JEREMY. I think somebody still comes here.

MICHAEL. Why?

JEREMY. Well..I mean...those empty cans don't look
as if they've been here too long. There's stuff all
over the place.

MICHAEL. Shite!....wait a minute....what kind of
nutter eats cold tins of beans in a cold draughty

hut? Look at those rags, who'd kip in that...
they'd have tae be mad.

MICHAEL points his gun towards the door

MICHAEL. It's probably a tramp....well he better no
turn up the night...for his sake.

Pause

MICHAEL. Have you been in this shack before?
JEREMY. Yeah, I used to get drill in here.
MICHAEL. Aye, I bet you did ya bastard!

MICHAEL spits at JEREMY

JEREMY. Sorry I didn't...
MICHAEL. Shut it!

*Pause. MICHAEL walks around the room
again*

MICHAEL. Has this place got a bog?
JEREMY. A what?
MICHAEL. Has it got a bog? A toilet?
JEREMY. A toilet?
MICHAEL. Aye, a toilet.
JEREMY. I don't think so...you could piss in that paint
tin if you wanted.

MICHAEL. It's no a piss I want.

Pause

MICHAEL. Right.....cigarette!
JEREMY. Oh, yes please.
MICHAEL. No...I mean....have you got a fuckin
cigarette!
JEREMY. I've only got one left.....you can have it if
you want.
MICHAEL. Aye, I do want......right ...stand up.

JEREMY stands up

MICHAEL. Right go over and put your hands against
the wall.
JEREMY. What?
MICHAEL. Go and put your hands against the wall.

*JEREMY looks puzzled, he walks backwards
to the wall, and puts his hands against it, still facing
MICHAEL*

MICHAEL. No like that ya stupid.....you taking the
piss?
JEREMY. No...no...honest.
MICHAEL. Dae it like they do on the telly!

MICHAEL makes JEREMY turn and face

the wall. Placing the palms of JEREMY's hands against it he searches him, going through all his pockets. He then throws the contents on the floor; except the cigarette packet. he takes out the cigarette and throws the packet away. He hands it to JEREMY.

MICHAEL. Light it.

JEREMY does as he is told. When it is lit he turns to face MICHAEL, taking a couple of puffs before he hands it on.

MICHAEL. Right, shut your eyes.
JEREMY. Shut my eyes?
MICHAEL. I don't want you to see my face when I'm smoking.
JEREMY. Oh come on!
MICHAEL. Just do it!

JEREMY sighs and makes a great show of closing his eyes tightly. MICHAEL looks at him and feels stupid.

MICHAEL. Aye, you're fuckin hilarious,...... just turn and face the wall.

JEREMY turns to face the wall. MICHAEL pulls down his scarf and takes a few puffs of the cigarette. When he has had enough, he pulls the scarf back up. He hands the cigarette to JEREMY

MICHAEL. Here, now get on the floor and shut up.

> *JEREMY sits in the middle of the floor smoking. MICHAEL paces around the room. JEREMY watches him.*

JEREMY. Look you can take that scarf off if you want.
MICHAEL. Don't be stupid....I cant take it off.
JEREMY. Why not?
MICHAEL. Because you'd see my face that's why not.
JEREMY. That's what I'm trying to say, I've seen your face already.
MICHAEL. What?
JEREMY. When you jumped me....I saw your face.
MICHAEL. You're lying.
JEREMY. You weren't walking around the streets with a scarf covering your face......were you? Anyway what difference does it make?
MICHAEL. It makes a big difference, it means you can identify me.

> *MICHAEL slowly pulls his scarf down*

JEREMY. Wait a minute....I wouldn't tell anybody ..I won't say anything...honest.

> *MICHAEL moves slowly towards JEREMY*

MICHAEL. You stupid fuck...you stupid...stupid fuck.
JEREMY. Sorry...sorry.

Points the gun at JEREMY

MICHAEL. I'm gonnae have tae shoot you.

There is a brief uneasy silence, then JEREMY runs screaming to the corner of the room

JEREMY. Oh no please ....please don't shoot me .... I won't say anything, I promise I won't .

MICHAEL runs over to JEREMY with the gun still pointing at him

MICHAEL. Hey shut up....shut the fuck up....

JEREMY still shouting

JEREMY. Please don't shoot me.......I saw nothing.. .....nothing
MICHAEL. Be quiet will ye?.....be quiet please...I won,t shoot you...I promise I won't shoot you.

There is a silence as MICHAEL breaks away from JEREMY

MICHAEL. Christ.....I was only kidding, can youse no
    even take a joke down here.

*MICHAEL thinks he hears a noise and quickly
turns, pointing his gun at the door*

MICHAEL. What was that? Did you hear something?
    ....did ye?
JEREMY. No ..I never heard anything.
MICHAEL. You could be lying....some of your
    squaddie mates eh?....fifty against one..."Our
    British boys done good"
JEREMY. What?
MICHAEL. A rescue...a fuckin rescue...just like the
    Iranian embassy.
JEREMY. What are you on about?
MICHAEL. Shut it!

*MICHAEL has the gun pointed at the door.
He listens for a while. There is no noise.*

MICHAEL. It might be that tramp....aye, well it better
    no be.
JEREMY. Look I wasn't lying....I didn't hear anything
    ...honest. Anyway..who'd want to rescue me.
    Nobody even knows I'm missing.
MICHAEL. Whoever it was has gone.

MICHAEL lowers the gun

MICHAEL. Fuck! Maybe they're away for
    reinforcements.
JEREMY. Oh come on!
MICHAEL. Shut it.

*He listens for a moment before realising no-
one is there. He puts more rubbish against the door
then turns to face JEREMY*

Pause

MICHAEL spots that JEREMY has a bag.

MICHAEL. What's that? What the fuck's that?

*JEREMY reluctantly hands over the bag to
MICHAEL. He empties the contents. There are sport
shoes, socks, football magazines, Gameboy, and at the
bottom of the bag, a portable phone. MICHAEL picks
it up.*

MICHAEL. What the fuck's this?
JEREMY. Eh...it's a phone.
MICHAEL. Aye I know what it is...but what's it doing
    in your bag? Ya fly bastard.....you were gonnae
    phone through for help...weren't you?
JEREMY. No I wasn't...I wasn't..honestly I wasn't.
MICHAEL. What's it doing in your bag then eh?

JEREMY. It's a present.

MICHAEL. What kind of a prick would give ye a present like that?

JEREMY. My father...he likes those sort of things.

MICHAEL. Your Da gave you that?

JEREMY. Yes.

MICHAEL (laughing). What a dickhead. Imagine giving somebody a phone...fuck; did he give you shares in British Telecom as well?

JEREMY. Well actually....yes he did.

MICHAEL. He's no just a dickhead..he's a pure dickhead. Did he no realise everybody would take the piss oot ye? I mean as soon as anybody takes one of them oot......It's like putting a sign on your forehead; "My name is prick".

JEREMY. He works away a lot. He told me it was in case of emergencies.

MICHAEL. Could you no just phone fae a phonebox like anybody else?

JEREMY. That's what I said........but he said it's so that he can phone me.

MICHAEL. And does he?

JEREMY. Well not really.....no.

MICHAEL (laughs). What a dickhead!

JEREMY. Yeah well he's always too busy.......always has been.

JEREMY looks at the floor. There is a short silence

18

MICHAEL. Hey look....I was only kidding around....he probably isnae a dickhead. At least he gave you something......all my da ever gave me was a good boot up the hole.

Pause

MICHAEL. What about your Ma?
JEREMY. Dead.
MICHAEL. Same here.
JEREMY. Well at least that's something we have in common.
MICHAEL. Aye, the only thing.

MICHAEL looks at the phone

MICHAEL. Does this thing work?
JEREMY. I suppose so.............. I've never used it
MICHAEL. What?
JEREMY. I wouldn't give him the pleasure.

MICHAEL looks at the phone again

MICHAEL. Wait a fuckin minute....I could use this.
JEREMY. Help yourself.
MICHAEL. I fuckin will.....I'm gonnae make a phonecall ....now you just keep it shut until I'm finished ....right....right!

JEREMY. Aye alright.

> *MICHAEL picks up the phone. He is trying to get a dialling tone, without any success. The more he tries, the more frustrated he gets.*

MICHAEL. Oh shite....how does this work?......how
    can I phone 'the boys' when the phone disnae
    work?
JEREMY. Hey....calm down mate.
MICHAEL. Don't tell me to calm down.......I'm
    fucked off and I've got a gun!

> *MICHAEL stares at JEREMY. There is a brief silence*

JEREMY. I was just going to say....I could get the
    phone to work.....if you wanted to.
MICHAEL. Oh aye, and how are you going to manage
    that then smartarse. You're just after saying you
    huvnae used it.
JEREMY. But I've used me dad's....It's exactly the
    same as mine.

> *MICHAEL throws the phone to JEREMY*

MICHAEL. Go on then....make it work...move it!
JEREMY. I'm not going to help kidnap me am I!

MICHAEL walks towards JEREMY

MICHAEL. Oh I see, well. we'll have to come to some sort of arrangement then, won't we? See....if you get the phone to work..I won't blow your fuckin head off.

Pause

JEREMY. Well..... that sounds fair enough to me....I just hope it works..that's all.
MICHAEL. So do I pal, so do I.

JEREMY tries the phone and immediately picks up the dialling tone

JEREMY. There you go.
MICHAEL. Right shut up while I make my call.

MICHAEL starts to search through his pockets for a piece of paper. He throws down other bits of paper, and then starts to search his pockets for a second time.

MICHAEL. Oh fuck!...fuck!

As he continues to search

JEREMY. What are you looking for?

Still searching

MICHAEL. It's a phone number right!
JEREMY. Any number in particular?
MICHAEL. Aye, but I don't know it. I mean...I wrote
    it down. Shite...this always happens to me....I
    wrote it down.

> *JEREMY looks through the papers with no*
success

JEREMY. It's not there.
MICHAEL. I know it's not there.
JEREMY. Who was it?

Pause

MICHAEL. The IRA.
JEREMY. What?
MICHAEL. I was gonnae phone the IRA ....tell then
    I've kidnapped a Brit.

Long Pause

JEREMY. I'm not trying to be cheeky....but I thought
    the IRA were Irish.
MICHAEL. Of course they are.

Pause

JEREMY. But I thought you were a jock.
MICHAEL. What!
JEREMY. I thought you were a jock...scotch like.
MICHAEL. Don't you ever call me that again. My
    Granda told me about the way the Scottish treated
    him, "No Irish need apply". He had to clean
    sewers oot wi his bare hands ....his bare hands
    ....him and the rest of the 'Stinking Irish". I'm a
    freedom fighter, I'm going to help free Ireland
    .....except I've lost their number.

Brief silence

JEREMY. So...you're......you're in the IRA then?
MICHAEL. Well I huvnae exactly joined yet...that
    was what I was going to phone them about....prove
    myself to them first.
JEREMY. I'd have thought it might have been pretty
    difficult to contact them, just like that.
MICHAEL. Aye, well...your precious army didnae
    have the contacts I have.
JEREMY. Contacts?
MICHAEL. Aye, contacts. Nae names right!

Pause

MICHAEL. My wee cousin knows a guy that works wi

a guy, that's married tae this lassie, right, that's
pally wi the wife of this guy whose uncle was in
the IRA ....in the early days like ....aye, high up
he wis tae. So he got it for us .....see.

JEREMY. Right.....and I can see how that might
confuse the army right enough.

MICHAEL. But what the fuck does it matter now ...the
number's lost.

JEREMY. What if they don't want you?

MICHAEL. Of course they'll want me ...they need
things like this to keep the cause in the public
eye.....I'll just have to think of another way of
contacting them that's all.

Pause

JEREMY. Well if it's publicity you want why not
phone a newspaper?

MICHAEL. Oh Aye, I'm just gonnae tell everybody
exactly where I am. Do you think I'm stupid?

JEREMY. No, but you don't have to tell them where
you are....just tell them what you've done.

MICHAEL. What?

JEREMY. Don't say who or where you are...... just say
you've got a hostage.

MICHAEL. Hey that's no bad....what's the nearest
paper tae here?

JEREMY. The Livepool Echo.

MICHAEL. What's their number?

JEREMY. I don't know but you could phone directory enquiries.
MICHAEL. Do it.

JEREMY picks up the phone and dials.

JEREMY. Hello...could I have the number of the Echo please?.....(to MICHAEL) Which department do you want?
MICHAEL. Well it's no the sport's department is it? The newsroom ya dickhead.
JEREMY. Could I have the newsroom please..thank you...there you go.
MICHAEL. Hello...hello.....is that the newsroom?..aye well you'd better listen, this is the IRA, I've kidnapped a British soldier.
JEREMY. What! I'm not a ...

MICHAEL points the gun at JEREMY

MICHAEL. Shut your mouth...what? No I don't have a fuckin codeword....No I'm not Scottish...I'm Irish. Look I've kidnapped a British soldier, his name is ...what's your name?
JEREMY. Jeremy........Jeremy Smith.
MICHAEL. Jeremy! Christ......his name is Jeremy Smith. Stop laughing.....this is serious, I've got a gun....I could blow his head off at any time.

JEREMY is becoming increasingly agitated

MICHAEL. No, it isnae a wind up, I could kill him now (*He aims at JEREMY*) start screaming!
JEREMY. What?
MICHAEL. Scream!

JEREMY starts screaming

MICHAEL. See this isnae a kid-on.....shite, he's hung up....the wanker's hung up.

JEREMY is still screaming

MICHAEL. You can shut up now.....I said you can shut up! What do they want? Do they want me to shoot you before they'll believe me?

JEREMY starts to shout at MICHAEL

JEREMY. What am I doing here? What am I doing here? I've done nothing to you and you're trying to kill me! You are a nutter, a bloody nutter, I haven't done anything.

JEREMY runs to the barricade and shouts outside

JEREMY. Help me, somebody help me. Please get me

out of here!

MICHAEL runs towards him

MICHAEL. Shut up, shut up. (*begins to panic*) ....be
quiet please...(*pointing the gun at JEREMY*) look
don't force me.....I don't want to do this.
JEREMY. Go on then shoot me, bloody shoot me! (*He
moves towards MICHAEL*) I don't care any more;
go on do it!
MICHAEL. Stop it!
JEREMY. Go on, you can't , can you? You've got no
intention of killing me ....have you? You haven't
got the guts, you're as much a coward as I am.
MICHAEL. I'm no a coward, don't call me a coward.

*He lunges at JEREMY they struggle on the
floor. JEREMY tries to get the gun. In the struggle the
gun is fired. JEREMY jumps away in terror. MICHAEL
stands up and points the gun at him*

MICHAEL. Shut up, shut up or I'll blow your fuckin
head off. (*He paces around the room*) Oh no, oh
no, the whole of bloody Liverpool will have
heard that. Oh god.......god.

There is a short silence

MICHAEL. What did you do that for? I wasn't gonnae

do anything. Oh Christ.

Pause

JEREMY (quietly). I just don't know why you've got
me here that's all.

MICHAEL. You're a British soldier.

JEREMY. What?

MICHAEL. You're a British soldier. Every Brit. is a
target. You are a prisoner of the freedom fighting
Irish Republican Army.

JEREMY. I'm not a British soldier.

MICHAEL. I know you're a soldier so shut your lying
British mouth.

JEREMY. Honest I'm not.

MICHAEL. You've got a British soldier's uniform on.

JEREMY. It's not a soldier's uniform...please believe
me.

MICHAEL. Alright, alright.....it's not a soldier's
uniform, what is it then?.....Answer me!

JEREMY. I'm a......a...

MICHAEL. A what?

JEREMY. I'm a cadet.

MICHAEL. A cadet?

JEREMY. Yes....a cadet.

MICHAEL. A cadet...-well that means you're training
to be a soldier, doesn't it?

JEREMY. No it doesn't.

MICHAEL. You're training to oppress people, aren't

you?

JEREMY. Me? I've never oppressed anyone in me life!

MICHAEL. Alright tell me what a cadet does then. What do you do?

JEREMY. Well I hardly ever go. Mrs. Ledwith lives near the hall, I usually go and see her.

MICHAEL. Who the fuck is Mrs. Ledwith?

JEREMY. She was a good friend of me mam's. She tells me things....things that happened.....good times .....know what I mean?

MICHAEL. No......I don't have a clue what ye mean.

JEREMY. She makes me feel like I'm near her...you know....me mam. I just cut the grass sometimes ...then she makes me tea....we just talk that's all.

MICHAEL. What is this...Songs of Fucking Praise? That sentimental shite won't work on me. "A volunteer must not become personally involved" ..that's what ma Granda said. What happens when ye *do* go eh?

JEREMY. Nothing really.

MICHAEL. You're getting on ma tits....what happens?

JEREMY. Well usually I just sit there, cos I can't stand it. I hate marching around like a prat and calling these secondary school heroes **sir!** They're the type that try out military manoeuvres on their Sega gamesThey've got Airfix aeroplanes hanging from their bedroom ceilings and have Lego tanks on their bedside cabinets, they can't sleep at night unless theyhave action man in beside them; in full military uniform of course. The only time they have fun is during their initiation ceremonies when they get to shave the hair off someone's balls; some poor sod that didn't even want to be there in the first place.

Pause

MICHAEL. What's wrong wi Airfix aeroplanes?
JEREMY. Oh hey....you didn't.....did you?
MICHAEL. Aye well, I was quite young.
JEREMY. And what did your Grandad think of that?
MICHAEL. What's that got tae do wi ma Granda?
JEREMY. Well it's not very patriotic is it? I mean how many bomber planes have the IRA got? You must have been doing British ones.
MICHAEL. I wis only aboot seven .....I didnae know the difference.
JEREMY. Until your Grandad taught you.
MICHAEL. Exactly....until ma Granda taught me.

Pause

MICHAEL. If you hate these cadets so much, why did ye join them in the first place?
JEREMY. It wasn't through choice, believe me. I suppose you could say I was called up.
MICHAEL. Aye right, you don't get called up these days.

JEREMY. No but me father called me up. He made me
join, said it would give me discipline, it would
toughen me up.
MICHAEL. Could you no just have said you didnae
want to go?
JEREMY. It was for punishment.
MICHAEL. What for?
JEREMY. I stole his credit cards.
MICHAEL. What? Are you crazy man?
JEREMY. I didn't use them. I just threw them down
the drain.
MICHAEL. What was the point of that?
JEREMY. There was no point, that was the point. I just
wanted to see the look on his face when he
realised his whole world was down the fuckin
drain.
MICHAEL. Did he give ye a right battering?....ma da
would have killed me.
JEREMY. No he sent me to my room as usual, didn't
speak to me at all. Then a few days later, he
presented me with a cadet's uniform. He had
everything arranged, said it would make a man of
me. Said it was about time I started to pay him
back, time to make him feel proud instead of
ashamed.
MICHAEL. Look I don't want to get into yer family
problems here, I've got problems enough of my
own. I've got a job to do...anyway how do I know
if you're telling the truth or not?......this could all

be lies just tae confuse me.

JEREMY. Honest, it's not lies......I..

MICHAEL. Shut it, you're still a Brit., every Brit's a
target.

Pause

JEREMY. You're a Brit.

MICHAEL. Am I fuck.

JEREMY. You are.

MICHAEL. Am I fuck!

JEREMY. Where were you born?

Pause

JEREMY. Where were you born?

MICHAEL *(reluctantly)*. Glasgow.

JEREMY. And where's that?

MICHAEL. Scotland.

JEREMY. And where's that? -Britain. You are a Brit.

MICHAEL. Do you want tae know how British I am?
You can stuff your Queen and your Union Jack
right up your arse. That's how British I am.

JEREMY. But you were born here. You must be
British.

MICHAEL. Is that right smartarse. Well if you were
born in a stable it doesn't mean you're a horse
does it? That's what ma Granda used to say.

JEREMY. Horses don't need passports....you do. If

you want to go anywhereyou'll need a British passport.

MICHAEL. I had no choice but to be born here.

JEREMY. You're not alone there mate. Not many people get to choose the place of their birth --if they did half of Liverpool would be born in Anfield , and the other half in Goodison Park.

MICHAEL. Shut it. Your lot made us come here. You bastards starved us out.

JEREMY. What do you mean "you bastards"?

MICHAEL. I mean you, you English Protestant bastards. You made us eat grass.

JEREMY. I don't know what you're talking about.

MICHAEL. I'm talking about the famine of 1845. You made us starve. You exported our food and we had to eat grass.

JEREMY. 1845! That's over a hundred years before I was born.

MICHAEL. So what? You're just a different generation of the same machine. You hate the Irish, but it's not because of the Troubles, not because of your fear of the IRA, it's because you feel guilty. So you try to push them aside ..to make fun of them "Did you hear about the thick Paddy that did this, the stupid Mick that did that." Well have **you** heard about the stupid Irishman that got tae thinking about all this, and then thought, well **fuck you!**

He shouts the last of this and points the gun at JEREMY. MICHAEL then sings the three following excerpts, each one in a more aggressive manner than the previous.

MICHAEL.
        For I've always hated slavery
        Since the day that I was born
        So I'm off to join the IRA
        And I'm off tomorrow morn

        So we're off to Dublin in the green
                fuck your Queen
        where the helmets glisten in the sun
                fuck her son
        where the bayonets slash
                your orange sash
        to the echo of the Thompson gun.

By the end of this third section MICHAEL has absolute hate in his voice. He sings this last section more quietly, but still with menace.

        oh no prods at all
        no sashes to sadden my eyes
        Mountbatten is deid
        we blew aff his heid,
        fuck yer queen and yer twelfth of July

MICHAEL holds the gun at JEREMY's head for a couple of seconds then paces around the room. JEREMY is terrified, but after a pause he speaks.

JEREMY (quietly). I don't understand.

MICHAEL. It makes me laugh when you English pretend to be horrified by the Nazis. England was the first Nazi -to Ireland. You starved us.

JEREMY. I don't know what you're talking about, I don't understand.

MICHAEL. That's your problem, none of you understand.

Silence

JEREMY. Have you ever eaten grass?

MICHAEL. What?

JEREMY. I said have you ever....

MICHAEL. I heard what you said, ya cheeky shite. Of course I've never eaten grass.

JEREMY. Why does it bother you so much then?

MICHAEL. It's the thought, the thought of all those men and women, crawling on their bellies, fighting each other for food. My people starved, and you lot just sat back.

Silence

JEREMY. All that's still happening just now, and not just in Ireland.

MICHAEL. What?

JEREMY. People all over the world are crawling on their bellies for food, when there's more than enough to feed them.

MICHAEL. That's different.

JEREMY. How is it different?

MICHAEL. It's too far away. I was talking about Ireland. What can I do about it when it's so far away.

JEREMY. You can do far more than I can do for the people who died over a hundred years ago.

MICHAEL. I'm only one person, I can't help it. I'd like to help, but I don't want to feel guilty every time I eat my dinner.

JEREMY. Do you?

MICHAEL. Aye, sometimes....you're twisting things. It was just across the water not across the other side of the world.

JEREMY. It might as well have been unless you see it before you. Unless it directly affects you or your loved ones you'll feel bad, wish you could help, but do nothing. Not much has been learned since 1845, has it?

MICHAEL. But it has directly affected me, that's why I'm here.

JEREMY. Oh come on, every day you see this now. Every day I see some young lad willing to die for his cause. Don't you watch TV? Croat versus Serb versus Muslim versus Jew versus Palestinian .....Irish versus Irish. Don't you think they all think they're right? I mean god must have a multiple personality if he's on everyone's side.

MICHAEL. You don't understand.

JEREMY. Too right I don't....where is it going to end? When will it all stop?

MICHAEL. It'll never stop...It's in my blood!

JEREMY. You still don't get the point.

MICHAEL. Aye, I do get the point, but I'm here for a reason...and you'll never stop me. And remember, I'm kidnapping you, you're not kidnapping me .....so shut it!

Silence
MICHAEL takes a half eaten roll from his pocket and begins to eat it. JEREMY looks at him but when he catches MICHAEL's eye he looks away. This happens three times, then........

MICHAEL. Are you hungry?

JEREMY. I'm starving.

MICHAEL. Here. (*He throws him the rest of the roll*)

JEREMY. Ta, thanks (*he eats the roll*) how many times have you been to Ireland?

MICHAEL (*slight pause*) I haven't.

JEREMY. Never?

MICHAEL. ......ma Granda promised to take me.....but

he never got the chance. It doesn't mean I don't know anything about it.

JEREMY. You must have loved your grandfather ....to try to be what he wanted.

MICHAEL. I know what's right that's all....god this place stinks, what makes it stink so much?

JEREMY. Condensation.

MICHAEL. Condensation?

JEREMY. Condensation. You're in the docklands now mate.

MICHAEL. Docklands? It didn't look much like docklands to me when I dragged you past all those posh houses.

JEREMY. Oh that's the museum you're thinking about.

MICHAEL. You've got a museum in your docklands?

JEREMY. It's because it's near the city centre.

MICHAEL. The city centre. Is that where you get the boat to Ireland?

JEREMY. No, you need to get a bus.

MICHAEL. Don't take the piss -how can I get a bus to Ireland?

JEREMY. I mean you'll have to take the bus to the ferry.

MICHAEL. But we passed the ferry on the way here.

JEREMY. That's the Birkenhead ferry.

MICHAEL. Does it go to Ireland?

JEREMY. No....it goes to Birkenhead.

MICHAEL. Shite, I took you here because I thought I

was near the ferry, I thought I'd make a quick get away.

Pause

JEREMY. After you'd shot me, you mean.
MICHAEL. No I didn't mean that, after I'd tied you up.....blindfolded and gagged ye.
Pause

JEREMY. Where's the rope then? Where's the blindfold?

JEREMY stands up

JEREMY. You don't have to lie..you're planning to shoot me.
MICHAEL. No I'm not...I mean I will if you give me reason to.....don't get me wrong. But I'm not planning anything, I'm just doing my duty.
JEREMY. What did you think would happen here? You must have known.
MICHAEL. I don't know anything, I've never done this before, I don't know what I'm supposed to do.
JEREMY. Well that's very reassuring.
MICHAEL. But I won't ...I won't shoot you....unless you make me.
JEREMY. But what if you think I'm making you when

I'm not? What if you shoot me because of a
misunderstanding?

MICHAEL. I won't.

JEREMY. But what if you think I'm trying to get at you
when I'm not? How will you know?

MICHAEL. I know that you're starting to get there
now.....so shut it!

Silence

MICHAEL. Have you got a newspaper?

JEREMY. What?

MICHAEL. Do.....you......have......a.....newspaper?

JEREMY. No I haven't had the chance....I'll go and get
one for you if you like.

MICHAEL. Aye, very funny...never mind.

JEREMY. No I mean it. I'd come back with it....

MICHAEL. Aye and a hundred polis as well, I don't
think I'll bother.

JEREMY. I told you I'd come back, and I mean it
....anyway it won't be in yet.

MICHAEL. What are you on about of course it'll be in,
it must be after seven o clock by now.

JEREMY. But you didn't get through, they don't even
know I'm missing yet.

MICHAEL. I'm not talking about this ya clown.....I
want to find out the score.

JEREMY. The score about what?

MICHAEL. The football score...the big game was on

this afternoon.

JEREMY. Oh is that all....it was 2 - 2.

MICHAEL. Was it? How did you find out about that?

JEREMY. I saw it on the TV before I came out.

MICHAEL. Aye well, that's no a bad result, we were away from home. As long as we don't get beat eh?

JEREMY. Apparently it was an exciting match. It was 0 - 0 at half time. Then it was 1 - 0, 1 - 1, then with ten minutes to go 2 - 1, but the equalizer came in the last minute.

MICHAEL. Do you know who scored?

JEREMY. Yeah, Rush got two and Cottee got two. Julian Dicks and Neil Ruddock got sent off.

Pause

MICHAEL. That's Liverpool and Everton ya dickhead ..... I meant us against the Huns.

JEREMY. Pardon?

MICHAEL. The big game....Celtic v Rangers.

JEREMY. Oh I see..sorry...of course. I did see it, one of then won 5 - 1.... I'm not sure which one though.

Pause

MICHAEL. Oh that's brilliant....fuckin great. I bet they won it the bastards...five penalties.

JEREMY. I take it you support Rangers or Celtic then?

MICHAEL. Are you stupid....I'm Celtic daft....I hate
the Huns.

JEREMY. I don't know what all the fuss is about. I
mean I want Everton and Liverpool to win....they
just wear different colours..that's all.

MICHAEL. Celtic are Tims -Catholics, Rangers are
Huns -Protestants.

JEREMY. I thought all that had changed....didn't Mo
Johnston play for both teams....and he's a Catholic
...isn't he?

MICHAEL. He's a Judas bastard. He doesn't know
what he is!

JEREMY. He didn't do to well down here.

MICHAEL. I used to like Everton, now I hate them
because of that wee bastard....and I hate
Liverpool because of that arsehole Souness.

Pause

JEREMY. It seems to me ....you just hate people
because of religion -sort of defeats the purpose
..doesn't it?

MICHAEL. It's not the religion I hate, it's the history,
the history of oppression of Catholics in Ireland
and Scotland. It's happened for centuries, that's
why Catholics have to have their own schools,
that's why Rangers always have twelve men when
they play against Celtic, see, it's history that's
important.

JEREMY. Twelve men?

MICHAEL. Aye.....the referee's always on their side.

JEREMY. I'm sorry but that sounds more like paranoia than history

MICHAEL. Aye that's easy for you to say, you weren't brought up in it.

JEREMY. Look you come from Glasgow....not Belfast.

MICHAEL. It's just the same; except there's no guns.

JEREMY. Apart from you..eh?

MICHAEL. Aye.....apart from me.

Pause

JEREMY. You confuse me, one minute you're talking about people starving, about them eating grass, the next it's about football Catholic v Protestant. Why are you doing this?

MICHAEL. I am an IRA man but it's them that me do it.

JEREMY. You always seem to have a 'them', have you ever thought that you might be to blame as well?

MICHAEL. You never saw it. They spat on me. They'd wait at my bus stop every night, screaming at me "Dirty Fenian Bastard", "Taigy scum". I was forced to learn their songs, -they made me.

He sings the song in a forced way as if about to cry

Hello, hello we are the Billy Boys
hello, hello you'll know us by our
noise
we're up to our knees in Fenian
blood
surrender or you'll die
we are the Brigton Derry Boys

If it was Black blood or Jewish blood, or any
other kind of blood, there'd be riots all over the
country. But it's alright to say you're up to your
knees in Irish Catholic blood...Aye well fuck off.
JEREMY. So they spat at you, called you names....so
what? I've been called names all my life. I've
been spat on...beaten up...so what..I don't hate
them ...I just feel sorry for them.

MICHAEL is pacing up and down

MICHAEL. Aye, but they don't hate you because your
Irish, they don't hate you because you're a
Catholic.
JEREMY. Yeah that's right...they just hate me....-no
reason, they just do.
MICHAEL. I didn't mean it like that.
JEREMY. It's true, since I was a lad I was always on
my own. I wanted to be. I thought all the games
, the pranks, the laughs.....I thought they were
dead boring. There were groups, little gangs, I

suppose, but they didn't interest me. You must remember groups like that, they always have a leader; then there's a pecking order after him, until it gets to the bottom, the one that gets slapped, the one that's always last, the one that always gets caught. No thanks I'd rather be on me own. The leader's always the one who'll fight, it doesn't matter that he's got a brain the size of an ant's; he can fight. When I got to my thirteenth birthday I was a veteran of kickings off these groups, it used to really annoy them because I wouldn't fight back. I'd just roll into a ball and take it, they soon got bored. You say you're hated because you're Irish, a Catholic, well at least you knew why. Most people identify with something, skins, raves, football, religion, even work, when they meet people outside their group it means they can't continue on automatic pilot talking shite for hours. They've got to think, to communicate. I don't want to identify with any group. I mean you hated me because you thought I was a soldier, what if I'd been a nice soldier?

MICHAEL. There's no such thing.

JEREMY. Yeah there is.

MICHAEL. There isnae, when you're a soldier you're
    expected to kill, you can't afford to be nice.

JEREMY.   You say you're a soldier, and you seem
    alright.

MICHAEL. That's different, I mean, I'm fighting for

a cause.......they're fighting for money.

JEREMY. Oh come on, I don't think you could class your average British Army recruit as a mercenary. Most of them are boys, leave school, go on the dole for a couple of years, anything must seem better than that, ...and the telly blares it out "Join the professionals, see the world".   What would you do?

MICHAEL. They know what they're getting into....they know.

JEREMY. Just like you eh?

MICHAEL. Aye just like me.

Pause

JEREMY. What are you going to do now?

MICHAEL. I don't know. I'm thinking.

JEREMY. What about?

MICHAEL. Nothing....I'm just thinking.

JEREMY. Listen, I'm starving.

MICHAEL. Tough!

JEREMY. Hey come on....this is stupid.

MICHAEL. I don't know....I'm thinking.

JEREMY. Look I'm not trying to push you, but I do think this is a bit pointless...

MICHAEL. I just need some time....(*he begins to panic*) No please....please don't let it happen again.......please..

JEREMY. All I'm saying is....the longer this goes on,

the more likely you are to be discovered. If it all stops now, no-one would know any different.

MICHAEL. I can't...I can't...help me granda....help me..

JEREMY. Look mate you're not a killer; you're just a bit fucked up that's all.

MICHAEL. I ....(*he says this quietly*) ..Granda ......Granda...

JEREMY. ...come on....

JEREMY moves towards MICHAEL . MICHAEL screams the word 'Granda' and points the gun directly at JEREMY's head. JEREMY scrambles backwards and falls down. MICHAEL stands over him with the gun at his head. MICHAEL breaks down and cries during the following speech. He recites it as he would a well known prayer. the whole speech is reproduced here, but it may be broken up such that only parts of it are recited at this point

MICHAEL. Granda...Granda.....Irishmen and Irishwomen. In the name of God, and of the dead generations from which she receives her old tradition of Nationhood, Ireland, through us summons her children to her flag, and strikes for freedom. Having organised and trained her manhood through her secret revolutionary organisation, the Irish Republican Brotherhood, and through her open military organisations, The

Irish Volunteers, and The Irish Citizens Army, having patiently perfected her discipline, having resolutely waited for the right moment to reveal itself, she now seizes that moment, and supported by her exiled children in America and by gallant allies in Europe, but relying in the first on her own strength, she strikes in full confidence of victory (*He looks at JEREMY*)

Pause

We declare the right of the people of Ireland to the ownership of Ireland and to the unfettered control of Irish destinies to be sovereign and indefeasible. The long usurpation of that right by a foreign people and government, has not extinguished the right and nor can it ever be distinguished, except by the destruction of the Irish people. In every generation the Irish people have reserved the right to national freedom and sovereignty; six times during the past three hundred years they have asserted it in arms........ Standing on that fundamental right, and again asserting it in arms in the face of the world, we hereby proclaim the Irish republic as a Sovereign and Independant State and we pledge our lives, and the lives of our comrades in arms, to the cause of its freedom, of its welfare, and of its exultation among the nations. The Irish Republic is entitled to and hereby claims the allegiance of every Irishman and Irishwoman. The Republic guarantees religious and civil liberty, equal rights and equal opportunities to all citizens and declares its resolve to pursue the happiness and prosperity of the whole nation and of all its parts, cherishing all the children of the nation equally, and oblivious of the differences carefully fostered by an alien government, which have divided a minority from the majority in the past. Until our aims have brought the opportune moment for the establishment of a permanent national government, representative of the whole people of Ireland, and elected by the suffrages of all her men and women, the provisional government hereby constituted will administer the civil and military affairs of the Republic in trust for those people. We place the care of the Republic under the protection of the most high God, whose blessing we invoke upon our arms, and we pray that no-one who serves the cause will dishonour it by cowardice, inhumanity or rapine. In this supreme hour the Irish nation must by its valour and discipline and by the readiness of its children to sacrifice themselves for the common good, prove itself worthy of the august destiny to which it is called! ..... sacrifice themselves ..... sacrifice themselves ....

*MICHAEL holds the gun at JEREMY's head
ready to shoot, but his hand is shaking violently. He
can't do it and he starts crying and sobbing*

MICHAEL. Sacrifice yourself........but I can't, can I?
I can't do anything right. Oh God, some IRA
man I am eh?......terrifying....the British Army
would quake in their boots at the very sight of
me.......

Pause

MICHAEL. ....you can get up...don't worry you
can go........just go..

*Silence. JEREMY, his eyes on MICHAEL,
stands up slowly*

MICHAEL. What's wrong wi you? I told you to
go...now fuck off before I change my mind.......fuck
off.

*JEREMY steps back but continues to watch
MICHAEL*

JEREMY. Don't worry, you'll be alright.
MICHAEL. What are you on about? Now piss off, I'm
not holding you here, you can go......Are you
stupid? Watch my lips...you can go...I won't

touch you...I promise.

JEREMY. I know you won't.

MICHAEL. Well...what's keeping you?

JEREMY. I'm not going anywhere.

MICHAEL. What?

JEREMY. Just shut up for a minute....and listen.

MICHAEL. You can't tell me.....

JEREMY. I said listen. When you dragged me in
here...at first I thought you were a loony ... Then
after talking to you for a while, I thought you were
maybe just a dreamer living out some fantasy.

MICHAEL. Aye well...you were right.

JEREMY. No I wasn't...I was wrong. see I don't give
a shit about anything.....If I believed in something
the way you do....I'd be happy ..who knows .....
maybe. I'd do what you have done. Some of the
things you said in that speech were beautiful. All
I know about Ireland is that they seem to keep
blowing each other up. I don't understand that, I
mean where does that get anyone? But you were
talking about dead generations, equal rights for
everyone ...I mean I thought they were fighting
just because they hate each other. But you said
there were six uprisings in the last three hundred
years, you'd think somebody could have got it
right by now ....I envy you ...I envy the way you
feel about this ..... I just think you've gone about
it the wrong way. You should go and visit the
place....see it, but don't let it rule your life.

MICHAEL. My life...what are you going on about....it is my life. Do you think I'd be here if it wasn't my life?

JEREMY. Of course not. I just think you should allow other things in your life......like having a laugh.

MICHAEL. Christ.....it's happening again. I am in a scout hut alone with a cadet, a fuckin cadet. I've got a gun in my hand, and even then I can't get you to do what I want. When I force you to stay you scream to get out, and when I tell you to go, you want to stay.....Then you give me a fuckin lecture about my life...my fuckin life... It's happening again, I'm getting told what to do again, getting reminded of how useless I am.... "Do something with your life, it's all stretched out in front of you"....shite....shite! I don't want it to stretch out in front of me...I   don't fuckin want it at all.

JEREMY. Hey come on...you don't mean that.

MICHAEL. I do...I couldnae take this much longer... but I wanted to go out with a bang, to make sure people remember me. Everybody I know has packed it in already, the only thing they look forward to....is an end to it all. So they stay out of their heads all the time, live to avoid living .. I just wanted to show them .... to show them ... to show myself ... that I was different, that I could do something right, something special. And I thought well, that would make it even better. But I can't even get that right.

Pause

JEREMY. You've nothing to be ashamed of, even if
     this doesn't work, at least you want to do
     something. All I ever do is run away ... every time
     I think I could face them ....I bottle out. ....
     One time right, I came home crying from school,
     everybody in the place hated me, but I'd tried this
     time, I really did try. There was this group who
     used to stand outside the toilets, I suppose they
     were a gang. Everybody was terrified of
     them, especially me, every time I passed they
     kicked the shit out of me. This day wasn't any
     different, as I walked past they pulled me in. They
     slapped me about for a while, and they stopped
     when they got bored. Their top man was Quinny,
     Big Quinny, he told me he needed me to do him a
     favour. I didn't trust him, but I thought maybe,
     just maybe if I did this favour they'd all leave me
     alone. So I said alright. He'd lost his ciggies,
     some teacher had come up the corridor, and he'd
     thrown them in the air vent. The problem was that
     no-one could reach them. So Quinny asked me.
     He took the air vent off and lifted me in. The
     funny thing is, I remember feeling good because
     they all started cheering me on, chanting my
     name. I saw the ciggie packet, it was half way up

the air vent, I shouted down to them, told them it was too far up......but they kept cheering me. I crawled on my belly until they were in my reach, I strained my arm trying to get a hold of them ... eventually I got them. I shouted down to Quinny, it was a great feeling, they all let out a huge cheer .... The next thing I remember was a light coming from the top of the air vent. At first I thought they wanted me to climb to the top ..... but it was too far. As I started to move down, I squeezed on the ciggie packet... there were no ciggies in it. I shouted down to them told them it was empty..but they were all laughing..they closed the bottom of the vent, they were trying to shut me in. I started to panic, I hate small spaces, so I scrambled up the air vent ..... then I felt strange...I felt warm,warm and wet at the same time.....they were pissing on me, pissing on me face, me hair and me clothes. I moved down the vent...it seemed like years before I got out...and it didn't stop....I think they must have been taking turns. When I got out, they were all waiting for me, laughing. I couldn't hear them, I couldn't hear anything, I could just see all those silent, shaking, open mouths. I turned to Quinny...I don't know why, but I held out the empty ciggie packet .... it was dripping .... me mouth opened and I heard myself say "There's no ciggies in this packet". Christ, they were all falling about by this time .... and Quinny looked at me and laughed. I wanted to kill them, but I couldn't move, couldn't speak. All of a sudden they all disappeared. Friel, the English head, was standing looking at me. He started screaming at me...looking at me with disgust .... with hate ... I ran away ... ran all the way home. The school had already phoned me dad. I was still crying as he opened the door, I threw myself into his arms ... I needed him .... and all he could do was hit me .... and tell me to be a man. He was ashamed because other people had abused me. Would he have been so ashamed if I had abused someone else? I wanted to kill myself .... but I didn't .... I wanted to kill them .... but I didn't. I didn't do anything. I left it alone. It became a story everyone knew at school, they all looked at me as if I was a bad smell, as if it was my fault ...... Me dad never spoke about it again, he thought I'd just forget about it .... No way! I've never hated anyone because of what they are. But I do hate people because of what they've done .... not three hundred years ago ...three years ago. I do hate them ... and I understand you more than you know. You haven't failed, you've just reacted .... There's nothing to be ashamed of ... nothing .... Anyway how can you say you're a failure? You did a pretty good job of kidnapping me.

MICHAEL. You think so?

JEREMY. Well I'm here aren't I?

Pause. MICHAEL stares at JEREMY

MICHAEL. They pissed on you ..... I can't believe
  those bastards pissed on you ...They must be
  animals. If they were here now I'd piss on them,
  I'd fuckin hammer the scummy bastards. Do you
  no want to get them back?.... I would.
JEREMY. I do...but I don't know how.
MICHAEL. What was that? What was that? Did you
  hear something?
JEREMY. OH God......this place gives me the shits.
MICHAEL. Why?
JEREMY. We're near the docks.
MICHAEL. So!
JEREMY. The docks, this is where they used to bring
  the slave ships. Thousands died here; I've heard
  all the stories...their spirits still haunt the place.
MICHAEL. Oh shite, don't say that...I hate ghosts.
JEREMY. It might be that tramp.
MICHAEL. If it's a tramp I'll blow his fuckin head off
  ... I'm not worried, whoever it is has to come
  through that door first.
JEREMY. Not if it's a ghost it doesn't.
MICHAEL. Oh shut up about ghosts....oh shit, I can
  definitely hear something. Go and have a look.
JEREMY. You go and have a look.
MICHAEL. Have a look I said...I'll stand right behind
  you.

JEREMY moves to the barricade and peers through

JEREMY. Christ! Get down, get down.

MICHAEL. What is it?

JEREMY. Someone's definitely there...I think it's the Bizzies.

MICHAEL. The what?

JEREMY. The bizzies...the police....

MICHAEL. Oh no...they must have heard the gun go off .... what'll I do now?

JEREMY. Get rid of the gun...hide it somewhere.

MICHAEL. Where?

JEREMY. Anywhere..just get rid of it....we'll say we were kidding around.

MICHAEL. Oh no, no....

JEREMY. What are you going to do?

MICHAEL points the gun at JEREMY

MICHAEL. Get your hands on your head!

JEREMY. What?

MICHAEL(*screaming*). Do it!

JEREMY. Don't do this...I thought we were mates now.

MICHAEL. I've got to...can't you see that....I can't give up this time.

JEREMY. Please...please don't shoot me.

MICHAEL looks at him for a second

MICHAEL. Aw fuck.....fuck!

MICHAEL points gun at the door

MICHAEL. When they come in here I'll dae them,
then they'll know I can do it. Tell them who I am,
tell them why...make sure they know.
JEREMY. Don't do it, please, it's not worth it...please!
MICHAEL. Get back.(*starts screaming*) Granda ...
Granda! ...... I will sacrifice myself for the common
good. I am worthy of the august destiny to which
I am called ....Granda!

Blackout. END OF ACT ONE

ACT 2

The ACT opens where ACT 1 ended. JEREMY is cowering in terror on the floor, MICHAEL has the gun pointed at the door. There is a noise as the door and the barricades are slowly pushed open. A YOUNG WOMAN enters. She looks wet and cold. She stops as she spots JEREMY on the floor. Then she turns and sees MICHAEL, who is looking at her, and still pointing the gun. She looks at both impassively. MICHAEL keeps the gun pointing shakily at her.

MICHAEL. Who the fuck are you?

      She continues to look at him without showing any fear

MICHAEL. Are you deaf? Who are you?

      She continues to stare at him

MICHAEL. What are you staring at? Stop looking at me like that. Stop it.

      MICHAEL walks up to her and walks around her

MICHAEL. Who are you? What are you doing here?

Are you a loony, what are you doing here?

She continues to stare at MICHAEL

MICHAEL. Christ, she looks mad, maybe she's a
    loony.

*JEREMY walks towards the WOMAN. She
stares at MICHAEL. She turns to look at JEREMY, then
moves towards a pile of rags in the room. She sits down
and covers herself with them. She reaches for the half
full tin of beans and eats them hungrily. MICHAEL
walks behind her.*

MICHAEL. Alright you're no saying who ye are ....
    but that's the last time you move anywhere in this
    room without my say-so. Alright..alright!

*WOMAN ignores him and begins to rock
gently. MICHAEL shouts at her.*

MICHAEL. Did you hear me? I'm in charge here ...
    I've got a gun, do you hear me...a gun!

*WOMAN looks at him with contempt, then
away again*

MICHAEL. I don't think you understand me, I'm
    desperate. I could end up doing anything. I'm

holding a hostage, now you've put yourself in the same boat .... Christ , she's right oot the game. She **is** a loony, a fuckin loony. Just when everything was going smoothly.

JEREMY. Smoothly!

MICHAEL. Aye well, things were a lot better than they are now.

JEREMY. What are you talking about? You were about to shoot me. I don't call that "running smoothly".

MICHAEL. I probably wouldn't have done anything.

JEREMY. You looked serious enough to me.

MICHAEL. Aye well, it's got a lot worse now hasn't it?

JEREMY. Why?

MICHAEL. Because now there are two of you. It was a lot simpler before. What am I going to do now?

JEREMY. What difference does that make? You didn't know what you were going to do before either.

MICHAEL. Don't take the piss.

JEREMY. I'm not, it's just the truth.

MICHAEL. Alright, alright, but if I didn't know before, it's double worse now.

Silence. After a few moments it becomes obvious that the WOMAN is silently crying.

MICHAEL. Maybe she's escaped from a hospital. (*loudly*) Were you in a hospital hen? .... a hospital? .... Christ, if she wisnae she should have been.

JEREMY. You shouting at her isn't going to help.

MICHAEL. Maybe she is deaf and dumb, I know a few phrases of that, I had to visit a deaf and dumb school when I was in the Junior St. Vincent de Paul. here hen.........

MICHAEL walks in front of the WOMAN and tries to communicate with her by sign language

MICHAEL. Well she's obviously no deaf and dumb, she would've understood that.

JEREMY. What did you say?

MICHAEL. Just a few phrases I learned.

JEREMY. Like what?

MICHAEL. They were the only ones I knew.

JEREMY. Go on!

MICHAEL. Well I started by saying "Do you come here often?" but she didnae even blink.

JEREMY. "Do you come here often?"! No wonder she didn't blink, if she understood you she probably thought you were the worst sign language chat up merchant in England.

MICHAEL. Can you do any better, at least I know a couple of phrases, it was worth a try.

JEREMY. What else did you say?

MICHAEL. I'm no telling you.

JEREMY. Oh come on, don't go in the huff. I was just

getting a laugh, go on.

MICHAEL. Well, when "Do you come here often?"
    didn't work I thought it would be better if I tried
    to bring attention to myself. So I said "My
    name is Caroline, what's yours?".

JEREMY bursts out laughing

JEREMY. What?

MICHAEL. Shut up ya bastard, it didn't matter what
    I said I was just trying to find out if she spoke
    sign language!

JEREMY. (*still laughing*) Sorry ..... Caroline ...... this
    puts a different perspective on everything.

MICHAEL. Shut it!

JEREMY. They will write songs about you after you
    die - "A boy named Caroline".

*MICHAEL gets angry and walks up to
JEREMY*

MICHAEL. I don't know what you're laughing at, you
    still stink of piss.

Silence

MICHAEL. I didn't know how to say my own name
    smartarse. One of the girls at the school was
    called Caroline ...... I just used to copy what she

did. I knew how to say **her** name but I never could remember my own.

JEREMY. What was the third phrase? I promise I won't laugh.

MICHAEL. Fuck off!

JEREMY. I said I wouldn't laugh.

MICHAEL. No, that **was** the third phrase, "Fuck off".

JEREMY holds in his laughter.

JEREMY. Well, you're right, she obviously can't understand sign language. I mean imagine a bloke walking up to you and saying "Do you come here often? My name is Caroline, what is yours? Fuck off!" You'd have to say something.

They both burst out laughing, there is no reaction from the WOMAN

MICHAEL. Well, at least it was worth a try.

JEREMY. She probably hasn't had any food for days.

MICHAEL. Aye well, she ate thae beans quick enough ... I was starving tae.

JEREMY goes towards the WOMAN

JEREMY. Is there something I can do to help? Look he doesn't mean any harm, he really doesn't, there's no need to be afraid.

JEREMY tries to touch the WOMAN's shoulder, but she pulls away

JEREMY. I'm sorry, I'm just trying to help.

MICHAEL. Leave her alone you never know what she might do.

JEREMY. Look who's talking.

MICHAEL. Maybe I could phone your newspaper now eh? -"Hello it's me again, your friendly IRA man, just to let you know, it wasn't a soldier I kidnapped; it was a cadet, and since we last spoke I've added a deaf and   dumb loony to the list". I can just see the headline now, "Deaf and dumb Heroine captures ruthless IRA murdering bastard".

The WOMAN laughs sarcastically at him

MICHAEL. Oh Christ, it comes to life. What were you laughing at hen? The fact that you're supposed to be deaf and dumb, or the fact that I'm an IRA man?

WOMAN laughs again and then stares at him

MICHAEL. See, look at the way she's staring at me! So the IRA are no tae your taste eh! Aye well I'm sorry but I'm an IRA man, I am fighting for freedom. "Ireland through us summons her children to her flag and strikes for freedom".

WOMAN spits at his feet

MICHAEL. Did you see that? That's what we're up against. I told you they're everywhere, the bitch is a Hun. She hates us... don't you ....don't you? Well I'm sorry to disappoint you hen, but some of us are willing to fight for what we believe in. Where do you come from? Why did you come here?

WOMAN continues to stare at him

MICHAEL. Stop staring at me...I hate folk staring at me. Stand up.....stand up. Jeremy, search her.
JEREMY. No chance!

MICHAEL walks towards WOMAN

MICHAEL. Stand up, I need to search you.

MICHAEL pulls WOMAN to her feet. As soon as he reaches out his hand to search her she lets out an ear-piercing scream. MICHAEL steps back. When he moves forward she screams again. He backs off.

MICHAEL. Alright....alright.....I won't search you.

WOMAN continues to stare at MICHAEL, then sits down in her own time

MICHAEL. I want her out of here, she's doing my head in.

JEREMY. You're both doing my head in .... look let's just get out of this. This is just getting out of hand.

MICHAEL. I can't go.

JEREMY. Why not? We can just walk out of here and pretend this never happened.

MICHAEL. Can we?

JEREMY. Yeah!

MICHAEL. And what about her? Where does she fit into all this?

JEREMY. What about her?

MICHAEL. We can't just leave her.

JEREMY. Why not?

MICHAEL. Because she hates me. As soon as we walked out the door she'd go to the nearest police station and report me.

JEREMY. Oh yeah, and what is she going to say, "Hello officer, I've just been in the scout hut with a mad Scotsman who's in the IRA, oh yeah, and he's with a cadet that he kidnapped at gunpoint .... they went thataway." She'd be the one they'd take and lock up....come on.

MICHAEL. No .....I can't

JEREMY. Well I've had enough....I'm going. I'm cold and hungry and this is beginning to lose its novelty value.

MICHAEL points the gun at him

MICHAEL. Sit down Jeremy.

JEREMY. Oh not again!

MICHAEL. Sit down.

JEREMY. Only five minutes ago you told me to go away, you promised you wouldn't harm me.

MICHAEL. That was five minutes ago.

JEREMY. I don't believe this.

MICHAEL. Now sit down Jeremy......I mean it. Look I know you wouldn't betray me but I need time to think ... sit down .....

JEREMY sits down

JEREMY. Just as long as you know I'm pissed off.

MICHAEL. Alright....

Silence followed by a slight lighting change where music or a song comes in. When the light returns MICHAEL is staring at the WOMAN. This sequence should convey the passing of time.

JEREMY. Permission to speak.

MICHAEL. Of course you can speak .....you don't
   need to ask.
JEREMY. Permission to move.
MICHAEL. Where do you want to go?

JEREMY sits closer to the WOMAN

JEREMY. Now that I know how things are, I may as
   well show some solidarity with my fellow victim.
MICHAEL. Alright I get the message. You can go in
   a minute, but you can't go straight home, we've
   got something to do first. I've got to deal with her.

WOMAN is staring at MICHAEL

JEREMY. Hey what's the something we're going to
   do? How do you know I'll want to do it?
MICHAEL. You'll want to do it alright.
JEREMY. What is it?
MICHAEL. You'll know soon enough. Give me your
   laces.
JEREMY. What?
MICHAEL. Give me your laces.
JEREMY. But I've got boots on ...... I won't be able to
   walk ...take your own laces.
MICHAEL. I'm going further than you. You can buy
   laces tomorrow. Now give me them.

JEREMY begins to undo his laces

JEREMY. Where are you going?

MICHAEL. I'm going to do it, I'm going to Ireland. I'll catch the ferry tonight.

JEREMY. To join up?

MICHAEL. I don't know. I'm going to Donegal. I'll visit my Granda's birthplace and see how I feel after that. I've only got ninety pounds so it won't be a long stay.

JEREMY. I've got my subscriptions for all my cadet activities, it must be thirty pounds .... you can have that.

MICHAEL. Would you do that for me?

JEREMY. Yeah..why not?

JEREMY goes into the inside of his shirt and brings out money

MICHAEL. Ya fly bastard!

JEREMY. If you're going to be an IRA man you'll have to do better than that. ....Here.

JEREMY hands the money to MICHAEL

MICHAEL. Ta.

JEREMY. What about your gun?

MICHAEL. What about it?

JEREMY. You'd better not take that on the ferry, if they found that on you, you'd get down straight away.

I mean they might search you at customs.

MICHAEL. You can have it.

JEREMY. What?

MICHAEL. It's yours. I'll give it to you after we get out of here. But you'd better promise to look after it, it belonged to my Granda ... it's ancient.

JEREMY. How did you know it still worked?

MICHAEL. I didn't. I found it among my Granda's things when he died.

JEREMY. I'll look after it.

MICHAEL. I'll still need it for one more fling before I go.

JEREMY looks at the WOMAN, then at MICHAEL

MICHAEL. I should have said we're going to need it.

JEREMY. We...what are we going to need it for?

MICHAEL. You and I are going to pay a little visit to chum Quinny and his mates.

JEREMY. Quinny! I don't know if that's a good idea.

MICHAEL. When we find him you are going to introduce me as your long lost cousin from Jockland. I'm going to bring up the fact that I heard through the grapevine that he likes to piss on people. Then I'll tell him it's a bit different in Scotland, we don't bother about people pissing on each other, but we do love to see folks shitting themselves. Then I'll pull the gun on him, I'll get him down on his knees, put the gun at his head, and tell him that if he so much as looks at you the wrong way I'll be back and I'll make sure he doesn't have anything to piss with. I'm sure he'll cooperate.

JEREMY. Do you think it will work?

MICHAEL. Of course it will, if some loony you didn't know threatened you with a gun you'd have to take notice .... just in case. He'll always be looking over his shoulder.

MICHAEL and JEREMY both laugh, then stop as they notice the WOMAN again.

JEREMY. What about her, are you just going to leave her?

MICHAEL. Give me your laces.

JEREMY takes off the laces and gives them to MICHAEL. He pulls them to test their strength.

MICHAEL. They should do.

JEREMY. What are you going to do?

MICHAEL. I'm going to tie her up with these.

JEREMY. You can't just leave her here. What if no-one finds her?

MICHAEL. She'll only be there for a while. After we've sorted Quinny out we'll go to the ferry. Once I'm safely on it, you can come back and let her go.

JEREMY. That's not a very good idea ..... she won't be too pleased by the time I arrive.

MICHAEL. Well you don't need to come back, just phone the police, they won't know who you are. Say it's anonymous tip and just tell them where she is.

JEREMY. Well, I suppose that might work.

MICHAEL. Right.

Both MICHAEL and JEREMY turn and look at the WOMAN

MICHAEL. Look we don't want to hurt you. just do what we say, and everything will be alright. You'll only be tied up for a wee while.

MICHAEL moves towards the WOMAN. He puts his hand in his pocket and takes out ten pounds. He offers it to her

MICHAEL. Look take this, maybe you can buy some food with it .... go on. .... Right just put your hands behind your back ... I won't tie them too tightly.

The WOMAN still sits staring at him. He reaches out to move her.

WOMAN. Touch me you bastard and I'll tear your balls off .... you too ya little shit.

     MICHAEL jumps back. He is shocked as is JEREMY, as much by the fact that she has actually spoken as by her distinct Northern Irish accent..MICHAEL moves back and stands beside JEREMY. He points the gun at her.

WOMAN. Nobody is going to tie me up, nobody is going to leave me here for the police to find, especially not you two pricks.

     WOMAN throws the rags down and moves around the room

MICHAEL. You ... you can't talk to us like that .... I've got a gun ... can you hear me I've got a gun.

WOMAN. Yeah, and it's only a small one, that sums you up, doesn't it? (*She turns and looks at MICHAEL*) You don't scare me, so you can forget trying to threaten me with your gun. And by the way, I'll talk to you whatever way I like.

JEREMY. (*whispers to MICHAEL*) What do you want to do now?

MICHAEL. I don't know you'll have to let me think.

WOMAN. That'd be a first ..... you haven't thought anything through so far. Now you better listen to me, you two will stay here until I decide otherwise.

It's me that's going to do the thinking.

MICHAEL. Wait a minute...you can't...

WOMAN. What are you going to do? Tell the IRA on me? Because you are well in there aren't you, you know all about them don't you? .....Don't make me laugh.

MICHAEL. I don't need to take this.

MICHAEL goes towards the door. The WOMAN stands in front of him

WOMAN. You make one move out of this door and I swear to god I'll scream rape.

MICHAEL pauses

WOMAN. I'll scream my fuckin head off. Who do you think they'll believe? -You with your gun......or me a defenceless girl three months pregnant? Think about it.

MICHAEL moves reluctantly back into the room

WOMAN. Not very nice is it? ... I'm talking to you ...... I said , not very nice is it?

MICHAEL. What?

WOMAN. Being kept against your will ... not very funny is it? Not very funny when it's someone else doing it to you. And see I'm doing it without a gun, maybe that's because I'm a woman eh? I don't need to prove how much of a man I am do I? (*She laughs*).

JEREMY. Look we didn't mean any harm ... honest.

WOMAN. Oh aye, tying up a pregnant woman wouldn't be doing any harm! Leaving her freezing on a filthy floor ... helpless,....wouldn't be doing any harm.

JEREMY. We didn't know you were pregnant.

WOMAN. Oh that makes a big difference does it? You'd have a clear conscience if it was anyone else? .... that's very thoughtful of you ..... Now why don't you two little boys sit there and talk shite while I do some thinking.

MICHAEL and JEREMY sit. There is a lighting change and music to mark the passing of time. The light returns to normal

JEREMY. Look, are we going to be here much longer?

MICHAEL. I'm supposed to catch a ferry.

WOMAN walks towards MICHAEL

WOMAN. Give me your gun...give it to me.

MICHAEL. No..it's my Granda's

WOMAN. Are you going to give it to me, or am I going to have to take it off you?

MICHAEL. Aye, that'll be right.

> *WOMAN launches herself at MICHAEL, screaming and slapping him about the head. They have a struggle. When MICHAEL pushes her back she doubles over and lets out a cry of pain. After a moment MICHAEL moves towards her.*
> *WOMAN springs up, slaps his head, and pulls the gun from MICHAEL's hand.*

WOMAN. You can stop shaking now .... you're quite safe ..... quite safe.

> *WOMAN sits down and points gun at MICHAEL and JEREMY. They sit up slowly and are obviously scared. There is another music change*

JEREMY. What are you going to do now?
MICHAEL. You've proved your point ... we're both shitting ourselves.

> *WOMAN continues to stare at them, and to point the gun at them*

JEREMY. Look, you can have whatever you want. Take the money (*turns to MICHAEL*) Give her the money, go on give it to her.
MICHAEL. I need it. What am I going to do without it?

JEREMY. I don't care. Give it to her.

MICHAEL. No I won't.

JEREMY. Give it to her and she'll let us go ..... you can't spend it here, now. Give it to her.

MICHAEL. No.

JEREMY. Give it to her.

JEREMY and MICHAEL start to fight each other on the floor. the WOMAN watches unconcerned. Eventually JEREMY sits on top of MICHAEL and has the money in his hand. He holds it out in the direction of the WOMAN. She stands up slowly. Walks over and takes the money, then returns to her place. JEREMY lets MICHAEL up.

MICHAEL. You were lucky , I slipped. I'll get you back for that. That's a hundred and thirty pounds you've just given her ya stupid bastard .... it wasn't yours to give. I ought to pan your head in .... .in fact I will.

JEREMY and MICHAEL start to struggle again

WOMAN. Stop it........(*shouts*) stop it!

JEREMY and MICHAEL stop fighting

WOMAN. You two had better behave yourselves,

there's no knowing what a woman in my condition might do. I'm supposed to have peaceful and relaxing surroundings. So no more cuddling on the floor; .... unless you've got any more money to give me.

MICHAEL. Fuck off!

WOMAN. Now, now a good Catholic boy like you shouldn't be using language like that. Are you trying to corrupt my unborn child, because if so I might just have to shoot you, ya little shit.

MICHAEL. I said fuck off ya bitch and I meant it!

JEREMY. Calm down. She's got a gun, remember.

WOMAN. You'd better listen to the Englishman, Scotty. Now apologise and we'll just forget it happened.

MICHAEL. I'm not going to apologise to you....and I'm no Scottish, I'm Irish, I'm more Irish than you.

WOMAN. Oh is that right Scotty? And where were you born?

MICHAEL. If you were born in a stable......

WOMAN. ....doesn't mean you're a horse does it? Not very original, you must do better than that.

MICHAEL. My Granda was Irish, I was brought up being Irish. I know more about Ireland than I know about anything else in the world.

WOMAN. Just like the Americans you mean ...... just like Noraid. They think we're a bunch of cheeky little leprechauns waging our cheeky little struggle against Basil Rathbone and the rest of those dastardly little Englishmen. They think Ireland is like John Wayne in The Quiet Man .... everyone's running about in horses and carts singing 'the Wild Colonial Boy', all the women look like Maureen O'Hara and they think it's perfectly fair for the man to beat the woman with a stick if she gets out of line .... maybe it's not all that far fetched.

MICHAEL. It's different for you, you don't want to be Irish, you want to be British. You are displaced, it's you that should be called Scotty. That's because you were all Scots who were forced to go to Ireland, That's why you're no Irish, you're different, dour, Presbyterian.

WOMAN. So you want a completely Catholic Ireland, do you? If you knew as much about your precious Ireland as you say you do, you'd know Protestants have been influential all the way through; Wolfe Tone, Charles Stewart Parnell.

MICHAEL. I've got nothing against Protestants, in fact, some of my best pals are Proddies.

JEREMY. Excuse me, I don't think this is going to get us anywhere.

WOMAN. (*to MICHAEL*) God you're so stupid... you're just like the rest of them. I suppose you are right in a way, you could fit into the scheme of things in Ulster just perfectly. I bet you'd be dragged off with the crowd, no mind of your own.

MICHAEL. I'd be proud to be dragged wi the crowd, if it was the Republican crowd. My Granda taught me a lot of things, and I'll do my best to remember them. One man's terrorist is another man's freedom fighter.

WOMAN. So it's back to your Irish Granda, it's him you want to prove yourself to. The blind leading the blind.

MICHAEL. You don't understand what it's all about. Alright ..... you might have been born in Ireland ..... maybe you know a bit about the Troubles .... but you're a woman, you don't know how things are .... you've got to fight back or you're dead.

WOMAN. What have you got to fight about? That's what I can't quite understand, you come from Scotland. Why in God's name do you want to fight for Ireland? Don't talk about fighting to me, I've had to fight every day of my life.

MICHAEL. Aye but I mean fighting wi my hands. When I was at school I had tae wait for a bus. By the time I got on the bus I was covered in spit. I used to walk away, but it didnae stop till I stopped it. And they did it because I was Irish, and a Catholic.

WOMAN. Spit can be cleaned off ..... blood can't, that's the difference. Where you come from it's all name calling, fist-fights...being spat on. Where I come from it's bullets and bombs. Can't you see Scotty, it's not pretend, it's real. Not stories and legends .... reality.

MICHAEL. Ach you're off your head. For someone that knows everything you're no doing very well are you?

WOMAN. If you weren't so sad, I'd be falling about laughing at you. Little boys and their fantasies, only you all turn into big boys, big boys and their nightmares .... I'm going to have to teach you a lesson Scotty.

MICHAEL. I don't need any lessons from you thanks.

WOMAN. Well it just so happens I think you do ... after all, you talk about all the things your Granda taught you. I think at least one lesson from me might be required to dilute the shit he put in your brains.

MICHAEL. Don't you insult my Granda!

The WOMAN holds the gun pointed at
MICHAEL

WOMAN. Fuck your Granda. Now you do exactly what I say or so help me I'll shoot you .... Believe me, I've nothing to lose ..... Right take your trousers off.

MICHAEL. What?

WOMAN. Take your trousers off .... and sit in the middle of the floor.

MICHAEL. That'll be right...no way.

WOMAN screams at MICHAEL

WOMAN. Do it!

MICHAEL stares at her. The WOMAN walks up to him and places the gun at his head. He eventually takes them off and sits on the floor

JEREMY. Me too?

JEREMY begins to undo his trousers

WOMAN. Not you English, you can go.
JEREMY. What?
WOMAN. You said you were cold and hungry, so go.
JEREMY. I can't.
WOMAN. Why not?
JEREMY. I'm not ...... I'm not leaving without him.
WOMAN. Such devotion ..... it's quite touching really
    ... Now if I get this right, he kidnapped you and
    kept you against your will. He held you at
    gunpoint, and now that you have a chance to go
    free ... you don't want to leave without him .... is
    there something wrong with you?
JEREMY. I can't.....he's my mate.
WOMAN. He's your mate! Oh boys and their mates
    eh? .... boys and their gangs!

WOMAN walks up to JEREMY

WOMAN. Well I'm sorry English but you'll have to go
... I've some business that I've just got to settle
with young Scotty here, your ears are far too
delicate for what I've got to say. Now get out!
JEREMY. No!

WOMAN points gun at JEREMY's head

WOMAN. I'm going to count to ten, if you're not out
of here by then I'll kill you .... I'm going to kill
him anyway (*pointing at MICHAEL*) so it won't
make any difference. It's up to you.
JEREMY. I can't just leave.
WOMAN. One...two...three...four
JEREMY. You can't be serious.
WOMAN. five....six....seven..
JEREMY. Okay..okay...I'm leaving.....I'll be back.

*JEREMY removes the barricade and exits
through the door. The WOMAN turns round to face
MICHAEL*

MICHAEL. He's not kidding by the way, he will be
back .... he'll go and get the police and bring them
straight here.
WOMAN. What's wrong Scotty? Are you scared?
What's it to you if the police come, surely it's me
that should be scared? .... but I'm not am I?

MICHAEL. What do you want?

WOMAN. I want to teach you Scotty, about little boys and the games they play.

MICHAEL. What are you on about?

WOMAN. You tell me.....you tell me why you are here .... then I'll tell you why I'm here.

MICHAEL. Why I'm here .... you'll never understand.

WOMAN. Alright I'll tell you why you're here. It all started with the famous Granda, him and stories of Oul Ireland

MICHAEL. I wanted to go to Ireland, that's why I'm here, and for your information I wanted to join the IRA. I wanted to fight for Ireland, to become a freedom fighter.

WOMAN. Little boys.......you all end up being little boys.

MICHAEL. What is all this little boy shite? I know how you're here anyway.

WOMAN. Oh is that right?

MICHAEL You came from some loony bin...you're off your head. I mean, who else would live in this dirty shitehole and eat cold tins of beans?

MICHAEL starts to laugh, then there is a long silence

MICHAEL. Oh what's wrong, don't tell me I've hurt your feelings. Are you houseproud or something?

WOMAN. I wouldn't worry about that Scotty, I have

no feelings left that you or anyone else can ever hurt.

MICHAEL. Do you want me to feel sorry for you now? .... Give me back my trousers and I'll think about it.

WOMAN. This is the beginning of your lesson Scotty. This is the story of little boys like you , how your dreams have become my nightmare.

MICHAEL. What are....

WOMAN. Don't interrupt. This is the time for you to listen, because if you don't listen you will never learn. And believe me, you must learn Scotty. If I do anything in my life I hope that just one of you will learn. You see, the difference between you and me is the difference between dreams and reality. In a dream you can always wake up, in a reality like this you never will. —The lesson begins on the 22nd of January 1969.

MICHAEL. What's so special about that date?

WOMAN. That, little boy, was the day I was born to an ordinary family, two parents, two brothers, and one sister. I was born in Northern Ireland, the country of your dreams, the land of your forefathers, in Derry to be exact. 1969 ... .apart from being the year of my birth was also the birth of the present Troubles. For every year of my life there has been an on-going war on my doorstep. for every week of my life, somebody has died because of that war. For every day of my life there is a young person who has left home, left a place they love to find a life without bombs or bullets. And for every minute of my life a tear has been shed by a mother for their son, or a son for their father.

MICHAEL. You can't have a struggle for freedom without casualties. That's the way it is.

WOMAN laughs gently

WOMAN. The family I was born to had a history, a history of being in the Troubles, one Troubles or another Troubles, there were always plenty to go around. I had a Grandfather who was involved in the uprising in 1916. Countless great uncles and cousins who fought on on either side in the civil war. And a brother imprisoned for being involved in the present day fight.

MICHAEL. Are you trying to say that you're a ...... you mean you're a Tim.

WOMAN. Born a Nationalist, a Republican, a Roman Catholic.

MICHAEL. Why didn't you say anything? You let me prattle on about you being a Hun.

WOMAN. Give a boy enough rope Scotty....

MICHAEL. My Granda fought in the civil war, maybe he knew some of your relations.

WOMAN. Maybe he killed some of them.

MICHAEL. I don't think so.

WOMAN. It was Irish killing Irish, remember?

Silence

MICHAEL. And your brother's in prison, where is he? Is he actually in the IRA?

WOMAN. My brother is in Long Kesh, he's been there since he was younger than you. And no he's not in the IRA, not the stickies, and not the Provo's. He was in the INLA. So he's on lists, Nationalist lists and Unionist lists. He will never have a moment's peace in the rest of his life. First part of the lesson, all my family are Irish, ancestors can be traced back several generations. I was born in Ireland myself, and have lived there all my life....So in fact, I am more Irish than you..... correct? .... correct?

MICHAEL. Correct. Aye alright .... correct. What are stickies?

WOMAN. Jesus you don't even know who you want to join. The stickies are the official IRA. Then you have the Provisional IRA or the Irish National Liberation Army. Who did you want to join Scotty?

MICHAEL. It disnae matter, they all want the same thing.

WOMAN. That's where you're wrong .... they all want different things, and they'd do anything to get them. It isn't all black and white .... right and wrong, Proddy and Tim. What's right about a joyrider getting kneecapped as a warning not to steal a car again? How can anyone justify that as Ireland's war? Now the second part of the lesson; the   difference between your dreams and my reality. You ran away from your home with a dream. You want to join the IRA just like others want to join the Foreign Legion. None of it was real, even the kidnapping, I mean imagine kidnapping a cadet....and then becoming mates with him! It's all a bit unreal isn't it?

MICHAEL. I suppose it is.

WOMAN. And me I ran away from home too. I had no choice Scotty; I was born where I was, I didn't choose. From the moment I was born there were people being shot, bombs going off, funeral marches, soldiers and jeeps all over the place. By the time I was old enough to know what was going on it didn't seem strange to me. It was what I'd always known, it was normal. It wasn't just on the radio or the telly, it was on the streets in the city centre. It wasn't happening to people from another country, it was round the corner, across the street, with people you'd heard of or knew. And part of it all Scotty, right at the very core of it all, on both sides, were boys like you.

MICHAEL. Like me?

WOMAN. Dreamers. Boys your age kill people .... they plant bombs. They fight for a dream, but people keep dying for it. Try to understand it's real .. real blood .. real pain. Widows are left, orphans are made, do you understand, try to understand, it's not pretend, there are no second chances.

MICHAEL. Why are you telling me all this?

WOMAN. Because it's time you grew up. You can walk away from this, and if you've learned anything you can start your life over again. It's too late for me.

MICHAEL. What do you mean?

WOMAN. What age are you Scotty?

MICHAEL. I'm nineteen, and by the way, my name is Michael.

WOMAN. Okay Michael, you're nineteen. I'm twenty four. Ireland and everything else has finished me, don't let it finish you.

MICHAEL. You're not finished, you said you were pregnant, doesn't that seem more like the start of something to you?

WOMAN. I've told you about boys and what happens to them, have you ever thought about the women? Who gets left to clean up? Who gets left on their own? Who has to cry night after night for their husbands and sons? I'll tell you what happens to the little girls when they get caught up in the world you and others like you create; they suffocate and die. I always meant to get away, I always had one travel brochure or another, I   used to study

them, plan where I'd live. You see that was my
dream,I dreamt of escape, not of causes and guns,
of just getting away. Can you imagine what it's
like walking down grey streets day after day,
looking at barbedwire,wondering whether it's up
there to keep you in or to keep someone else out,
trying to catch your breath, suffocating in a man-
made trap.I had a neighbour ..a friend really;
Peadar. He was like you ..... a dreamer .... just like
you. A stupid boy, and he had plenty of other
stupid boys to help him along.

MICHAEL. I'm no stupid.

WOMAN. What are you then eh? Jesus, you're all as
blind as each other. Bumping into each other in
the darkness, afraid your next step might be
your last, might be your final dare. You wrap the
flag around you boys ... why? ... Is it a comfort
blanket hiding all the pain, all the blood?

MICHAEL. You don't wear a flag to hide behind ...
fuck ... you show it to everybody if it's what you
believe in. If you're hiding it means you're
ashamed and I'm definitely not ashamed. Can
you not see how important it is? It is your life.
Nothing is more important than that and if your
friend saw his chance and took it ... plenty of folk
would think he was a hero.

WOMAN. And you're one of them.

MICHAEL. Aye ..I am......I'm one of them.

WOMAN. A hero...(*laughs*) oh aye very heroic.....

your hero ....There was I sitting on the back of the bus ..... I didn't even notice them. Four men ran   out in front of the bus ... scarves like yours covering their faces. The bus screeched to a stop ... the men jumped on. They told the driver to get off the bus "get off the bus ya bastard .. now ... now" For a minute I thought they were going to shoot him dead ... but they just pushed him off. Back on they came ..... the smallest one turned and pointed his gun at us "This vehicle is getting taken over by Volunteers .... now get off the fuckin bus" Jesus .. I had to stop myself from laughing, his voice was so high, he couldn't have been more than fourteen or fifteen ..... I looked at them ..... they all looked so young. There was something familiar about them .... especially the jumpy one, I knew him. I didn't look them in the eyes .. wee boys maybe ... but one wrong look and that wee boy might have to prove how much of a man he really is.

"Get off the bus .... get off the fuckin bus" they were screaming. I jumped up .... we all started to move, when this woman, this middle aged woman stepped in front of us. "Sit on yer arses" she said "There's no way I'm getting off this fuckin bus ... No way I'm walking up that bastard hill ... So yous can take yourselves off and steal another bus" they didn't know what to do, then the wee one says "I'll shoot ye missus, get off the bus or I'll shoot ye" the woman just stood where she was. "I know you ... I know all of yous, if yous want trouble, just keep going, you shouldn't shite on your own doorstep. If you want to take a bus, away up the Shankhill and get one" I couldn't believe it ..... they looked at each other. The jumpy one said "What the fuck now?" The wee one still had his gun pointed at everybody. The woman sat down again "Now get off the bus before I kick your arses". The wee one pointed his gun at her "Ya fat cow". Oh fuck, he turned and ran, they piled off the bus and ran away. It might have been funny ...... funny or pathetic, if it hadn't been so scary. I was so angry. Would he have shot me? Where would he have stopped? I told him I didn't want to see him again. But I did .... once .... it was too late, he'd been pulled in, he got caught up in it all. A few months later he was sentenced to ten years. That was when my trouble really started.

Peadar was alright, I liked him, as I said, he was a friend. But when he got put away everything changed. He thought I was his girlfriend and he told 'the boys' I was. One night I had a visit, I was told I was not allowed to go out with another man. I was told when I had to visit Peadar. I was given a prison sentence of my own. I did what I was told, I did it for two years. From jail to jail I trailed on my visits .... I felt as if I was more like forty than twenty.

MICHAEL. Did you sleep with him?

WOMAN. What?

MICHAEL. Did you sleep with Peadar?

WOMAN. What difference does that make?

MICHAEL. It makes a big difference, I mean if you slept with him you can understand why he thought you might be his girlfriend.

WOMAN stands up and shouts

WOMAN. You little bastard, you haven't understood a fuckin thing. Yes I did sleep with him, does that mean he owned me? I slept with him and because of that I spent two years being dead inside ... two years. Any man who looked at me was warned away, any man I spoke to was warned .... I had no life.

Long pause

WOMAN. I met a man, an Englishman.

MICHAEL. A Brit.

WOMAN. A man.....not a soldier, just a businessman. We helped each other, he was lonely and so was I. We saw each other on and off for six months. Then they found out, your boys found out (*she gets emotional now*). My hair was cut off with razor blades,then they cut me they cut my breasts, turned me into 'damaged goods'. They wanted to make sure no man would ever look at me again. Do you want to see? Do you want to see what happens when a dream turns into a nightmare? (*screams*) Do you?

MICHAEL. No ... no I don't .... look I'm sorry, I'm really sorry.

WOMAN. When I came round in the hospital there was a bag on my bed. It had my clothes, my birth certificate and my passport in it. I was told never to show my face again. Oh and it doesn't end there Scotty, it doesn't end there. I found out I was pregnant. So as you can see, it wasn't the start of anything, it was almost the end. I met my Englishman. He was embarrassed by me, he couldn't get rid of me quick   enough. Oh he was generous, he gave me money, he thought a termination was best in the circumstances. Sounds so bland doesn't it? ..... termination. Do you know what that is Scotty?

MICHAEL. Of course I do ... abortion ..... it doesn't mean I have to like it though.

WOMAN. Like it ? Where does liking it come in? You have no idea what it means,you have no idea what it feels like.

MICHAEL. When are you going to have it?

WOMAN. I didn't go through with it.

MICHAEL. Oh good ..... I think you've made the right

choice ... I find it hard to believe in ...... you
know, life is precious.

WOMAN. So it's precious when it's a foetus, but it's
all part of the game when it's a freedom fight?

MICHAEL. I never thought of it like that.

WOMAN. I didn't stop for your reasons. I didn't stop
because life is precious, I would never bring a
child into the world I know ... no .... I made a
decision. If the baby dies I want to die too.

Pause

WOMAN. Put your trousers on.

*MICHAEL gets up starts to pull on his
trousers*

WOMAN. Now go.

WOMAN gives him the money

WOMAN. I want you to remember the difference
between dreams and reality. Make a difference,
that's all you have to do.

*A noise at the door. JEREMY comes bursting
in*

JEREMY. The police are coming ... I phoned them ...

I swear to God.

MICHAEL. Shut up Jeremy, shut the fuck up!

JEREMY. Oh shit!

MICHAEL. *(to WOMAN)* Please, I want to help you.

JEREMY. Come on, let's get out of....

WOMAN. Get him out of here English, take him away.

JEREMY grabs MICHAEL out

WOMAN goes over to the rags and cover. herself. She looks at the gun and smiles. There is a slow blackout, followed by a gunshot.

Music

THE END